The Twelve Days of Christmas

A Celebration of Nature

Briana Corr Scott

NIMBUS
PUBLISHING LTD.
NIMBUS.CA

Nimbus Publishing Limited
3660 Strawberry Hill Street, Halifax, NS, B3K 5A9
(902) 455-4286 nimbus.ca

NB 1648
Printed and bound in Canada
Designed by Heather Bryan
Edited by Whitney Moran

Library and Archives Canada Cataloguing in Publication

Title: The twelve days of Christmas : a celebration of nature /
    Briana Corr Scott.
Other titles: Twelve days of Christmas (English folk song)
Names: Scott, Briana Corr, 1981- artist.
Identifiers: Canadiana (print) 20220265798 |
    Canadiana (ebook) 20220266689 | ISBN 9781774710968 (hardcover) |
    ISBN 9781774710975 (EPUB)
Subjects: LCSH: Folk songs, English—England—Texts. | LCSH: Folk songs,
    English—England—Pictorial works. | LCSH: Christmas music—Texts. |
    LCSH: Christmas music—Pictorial works.
Classification: LCC ND249.S3455 A4 2022 | DDC 759.11—dc23

Nimbus Publishing acknowledges the financial support for its publishing activities from the Government of Canada, the Canada Council for the Arts, and from the Province of Nova Scotia. We are pleased to work in partnership with the Province of Nova Scotia to develop and promote our creative industries for the benefit of all Nova Scotians.

This book belongs to

_____

_____

_____

On the first day of Christmas,
my true love gave to me...

A partridge in a pear tree

On the second day of Christmas,
my true love gave to me...

Two turtle doves

And a partridge in a pear tree

On the third day of Christmas,
my true love gave to me...

Three French hens

Two turtle doves
And a partridge in a pear tree

On the fourth day of Christmas,
my true love gave to me...

Four calling birds

Three French hens
Two turtle doves
And a partridge in a pear tree

On the fifth day of Christmas,
my true love gave to me...

Five golden rings

Four calling birds
Three French hens
Two turtle doves
And a partridge in a pear tree

On the sixth day of Christmas,
my true love gave to me...

Six geese a~laying

Five golden rings
Four calling birds
Three French hens
Two turtle doves
And a partridge in a pear tree

On the seventh day of Christmas,
my true love gave to me...

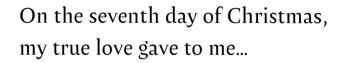

Seven swans a-swimming

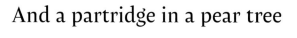

Six geese a-laying
Five golden rings
Four calling birds
Three French hens
Two turtle doves
And a partridge in a pear tree

On the eighth day of Christmas,
my true love gave to me...

Eight maids a-milking

Seven swans a-swimming
Six geese a-laying
Five golden rings
Four calling birds
Three French hens
Two turtle doves
And a partridge in a pear tree

On the ninth day of Christmas,
my true love gave to me...

Nine ladies dancing

Eight maids a-milking
Seven swans a-swimming
Six geese a-laying
Five golden rings
Four calling birds
Three French hens
Two turtle doves
And a partridge in a pear tree

On the tenth day of Christmas,
my true love gave to me...

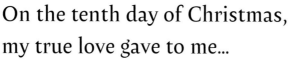

Nine ladies dancing
Eight maids a-milking
Seven swans a-swimming
Six geese a-laying
Five golden rings
Four calling birds
Three French hens
Two turtle doves
And a partridge in a pear tree

On the eleventh day of Christmas,
my true love gave to me...

Eleven pipers piping

Ten lords a-leaping
Nine ladies dancing
Eight maids a-milking
Seven swans a-swimming
Six geese a-laying
Five golden rings
Four calling birds
Three French hens
Two turtle doves
And a partridge in a pear tree

On the twelfth day of Christmas,
my true love gave to me...

Twelve drummers drumming

Eleven pipers piping
Ten lords a-leaping
Nine ladies dancing
Eight maids a-milking
Seven swans a-swimming
Six geese a-laying
Five golden rings
Four calling birds
Three French hens
Two turtle doves
And a partridge in a pear tree.

About the Images

Partridge in a Pear Tree

My own espaliered pear tree inspired the shape of the tree on the cover and title page. The pear branch is surrounded by amaryllis flowers, which grow from a bulb that is commonly brought indoors at the holidays.

Two Turtle Doves

The turtle doves on this page are surrounded by moths, dahlias, bright red roses, hand-drawn dragon fruit flowers and pomegranates. Pomegranates are in season from October to January, and in some countries are considered a holiday fruit.

Three French Hens

The French hens are surrounded by hellebore flowers created with ink, pencil, and oil paint. In colder climates, Hellebore blooms in early spring when the snow melts. In warmer climates, it is an evergreen perennial.

Four Calling Birds

The line "calling birds" was "colly birds" when this song was first sung. "Colly" referred to "coal," signifying a black bird. For my black birds I chose starlings, because they are ever-present outside my studio. The flowers shown are narcissus, or paper whites, which are fun to have bloom indoors in the winter.

Five Golden Rings

Some believe the "five golden rings" in this song referred to finches with bands of yellow on their neck, and others believe the gift of this day to be a ringed pheasant. In modern times the "rings" are depicted as jewellery, and it was hard for me to stray from that image. I decided to combine the two ideas by painting magpies with a hidden treasure.

Six Geese a-Laying

These geese are surrounded by Christmas cactus flowers, a beautiful plant that blooms around the holidays when kept indoors as a houseplant. This cacti's natural habitat is in Brazil.

Seven Swans a-Swimming

Seven swans are swimming (and two little ones are riding on their mother's backs) on an icy lake. I had to include pine cones and evergreen branches as a part of this holiday celebration. These pine branches were drawn from observation on my daily walks.

Eight Maids a-Milking

Recently, my family and l grew milkweed in our garden. We had our first monarch butterflies visit last summer. I couldn't think of a better image for "milkmaids" than this symbiotic pair. Bright blue clematis flowers are tangled amongst the milkweed.

Nine Ladies Dancing

Nine ladybugs play in tussles of echinacea blooms, mums, orange blossoms, Jerusalem flowers, and some seasonal clementines. Ladybugs are beetles, and can be male or female, but their name suited my illustration perfectly. They are a symbol of good luck, especially for farmers and gardeners because they eat harmful pests.

Ten Lords a-Leaping

My family cares for three pet rabbits. They are the little lords of our house, the ones we wait on and serve. I had to include our beloved buns as the inspiration for this page. In this image, they jump through giant artichoke flowers and young chestnuts.

Eleven Pipers Piping

Typically, this part of the song depicts bagpipers, or people playing wind instruments. Here, we have eleven sandpipers on the shore of a windy beach. One of the smallest seabirds, species of sandpiper can be found everywhere in the world, except for Antarctica.

Twelve Drummers Drumming

An imaginary forest of white birch and snow-sugared purple plums is host to twelve drummers: a flock of large woodpeckers called northern flickers. You will hear them drum on trees when looking for food. While illustrating this project, a flicker landed on my windowsill and begged for a portrait. She has since moved into a tree near my studio and is raising a family.

About the Song

The song "The Twelve Days of Christmas" is centuries old and believed to be a memory game played during a celebration between the 25th of December to the eve of January 5th. Frederic Austin is known as the composer of the modern version that we sing today, putting the melody to paper in 1909. My own family sings this song on long car rides en route from Nova Scotia to my childhood home in New Hampshire for the holidays. After many years and many rounds of resisting the ever-repeating lines, I realized that the imagery of the "gifts" in the song were just the type of thing I like to paint. As an illustrator who creates botanical-inspired images, this was a gift for *me*, and I dreamed of painting pear trees, partridges, calling birds, and turtle doves surrounded by flowers.

Once my imagination began to bloom, a beautiful, bountiful, nature-inspired feast for the eyes came to life. The lyrics of the song became a playground for me to find new meaning in ancient words. I paired the lyrics with unrelated species, both traditional and non-traditional flowers, and many varieties birds and insects.

I hope this nature-inspired version of an old song inspires you to create new traditions with the ones you love.

About the Author & Illustrator

Briana Corr Scott is an illustrator and author who lives in Dartmouth, Nova Scotia. She tells stories about the beauty of the natural world by creating hand-painted botanical illustrations, paper doll kits, and picture books.

Briana loves painting from life; she likes to hold something in her hand when she draws it, and she likes to see a place with her own eyes before she writes a story. She begins every writing and art project this way. Briana loves to make art about the overlooked details of the Atlantic coast. The underdogs of nature are a huge source of inspiration: weeds, moths, periwinkles, and fog are some of the star subjects in her work. Briana paints her botanical art with gouache and oil, then turns them into picture book illustrations, animations, wallpaper, and murals. Her stories are inspired by fairy tales and folklore. She has rewritten the tale of Thumbelina in her picture book *Wildflower,* and retold Selkie folklore in *The Book of Selkie. She Dreams of Sable Island* is a lullaby to a beautiful island off the coast of Nova Scotia. It is no surprise she has found inspiration in this centuries-old Christmas song.